PENGUIN BOOKS

LIFE'S LITTLE
DECONSTRUCTION

Andrew Boyd hangs his many hats at
www.wanderbody.com. He is the author
of *The Activist Cookbook*, a how-to guide
for cultural activists.

LIFE'S LITTLE
DECONSTRUCTION BOOK
Self-help for the post-hip
ANDREW BOYD

PENGUIN BOOKS

PENGUIN BOOKS

Published by the Penguin Group
Penguin Books Ltd, 27 Wrights Lane, London w8 5tz, England
Penguin Putnam Inc., 375 Hudson Street, New York, New York 10014, USA
Penguin Books Australia Ltd, Ringwood, Victoria, Australia
Penguin Books Canada Ltd, 10 Alcorn Avenue, Toronto, Ontario, Canada m4v 3r
Penguin Books (NZ) Ltd, Private Bag 102902, NSMC, Auckland, New Zealand

Penguin Books Ltd, Registered Offices: Harmondsworth, Middlesex, England

First published in the USA by W. W. Norton & Company Inc. 1999
First published in Great Britain in Penguin Books 1999

Set in 12.5/17.5 pt PostScript Filosofia
Typeset by Rowland Phototypesetting Ltd, Bury St Edmunds, Suffolk
Printed in England by Clays Ltd, St Ives plc

Acknowledgments

To Michael Barrish for his relentless editing and
uncommon friendship.

To Janice Fine for her shakabookoo in the sushi
bar.

To Liz Canner for her post-modern call to arms.

To Ken Jordan for his support and bulls-eye
counsel.

To Kosta Demos for his polymath generosity.

To Alane Mason for her patience, shared vision
and democratic sensibilities.

And to mom and dad for my initial encoding
and then some.

To each of you, I commemorate the following
imperatives, respectively:

279, 135, 295, 363, 144, 337, 10, 170.

1.

Talk about anything in the context of anything else.

2.

Implicate yourself in every interpretation.

3.

Dip into nihilism.

4.

Sample.

5.

Need what recently didn't exist.

6.

Expose depth as another surface.

7.
Pose.

8.
Control the remote.

9.
Read the text as you desire.

10.

Learn to play a financial instrument.

11.

Bathe in an image of the natural.

12.

Play each role in good faith.

13.

Publicize your privates.

14.

Pretend to be real.

15.

Fashion reason.

16.

Reason about fashion.

17.

Participate without belonging.

18.

Disenchant.

19.

Be as different from the Joneses as you can afford.

20.

Dissolve truth into a patchwork of language games.

21.

Indicate absence.

22.

Beg the question.

23.

Debt-finance immediate gratification.

24.

Resist – only to find yourself disarmed and reabsorbed.

25.

Inflate.

26.

Disdain theorists.

27.

Don't seek the whole.

28.

Confuse art and advertising.

29.

Replace your models *of* reality with models *as* reality.

30.

Sport amused, matter-of-fact
cynicism.

31.

Withdraw into shell-shocked blasé.

32.

Helplessly and forever, contain the
Other.

33.

Be as if.

34.
Reformat.

35.
Speak to be spoken – language
composes you.

36.
Manoeuvre between pastiche and
mishmash.

37.

Don't despair at the absurd, go with it.

38.

Regard conversation with the prestige
once reserved for inquiry.

39.

Perform your gender.

40.

Disregard the intentions of dead
authors.

41.

Supplant the original.

42.

Scrutinize power.

43.

Suspend belief.

44.

Write more about less.

45.

Complicate race.

46.

Shop as though money were a
consensual hallucination.

47.

Stake all on the charisma of the storytellers.

48.

Reduce meaning to a hodgepodge of signifiers.

49.

Enjoy plural sexualities.

50.

Lay claim to one fragment.

51.

Move laterally.

52.

Read provisionally.

53.

Repurpose symbols of power.

54.

Log on in search of community.

55.

Lip-synch.

56.

Beware: history speaks of goals never
intended.

57.

Voice subjugated discourses.

58.

Entertain alienation.

59.

Be a willy-nilly citizen of the world.

60.

Share nothing with strangers but an
obsession with celebrities.

61.

Refine your signal-to-noise ratio.

62.

Think where you cannot say you are.

63.

Without history, without heroes, rebel
against the blindness of information.

64.

Imitate Disneyworld.

65.

Learn from Las Vegas.

66.

Do something, anything, to attract
highly mobile capital.

67.

Rework what others have exhausted.

68.

Go digital.

69.

Go postal.

70.

Write texts that undermine their own authority.

71

Play the game.

72.

Dress as tourists imagine.

73.

Turn over your beliefs as fast as your assets.

74

Treat rationality as just another tradition.

75.

Profit from tastes you recently helped establish.

76.
Disorder taxonomies.

77.
Collapse hierarchy.

78.
Privatize truth.

79.

Question what belongs on the inside.

80.

Pursue multiple narratives that neither
explain nor unify.

81.

Cultivate decade-by-decade nostalgia.

82.

Show your work.

83.

Pose reality as an interesting
hypothesis.

84.

Help yourself.

85.

Think again.

86.

Schmooze.

87.

Take the kids to see a replica of what
never was.

88.

Be profoundly superficial.

89.

Cross borders.

90.

Negotiate identity.

91.

Look at, not into.

92.

Legitimate your own.

93.

Wallow in an orgy of information.

94.

Refer to what refers.

95.

Open up an abyss of infinite analytical regress.

96.

Rent a cop.

97.

Pass judgment without criteria.

98.

Be *ad hoc*.

99.

Name the ruling metaphor.

100.
Tweak your consciousness.

101.
Devalue.

102.
Remember: there are no facts, only interpretations.

103.

Edit the images you inhabit.

104.

Reinscribe what you can't surpass.

105.

Dismiss utopia.

106.

Live in a building that quotes other buildings.

107.
Speculate.

108.
Don't answer to a single standard.

109.
Trace meaning further and further
back.

110.
Let stories do their thing.

111.

Float globally, frame locally.

112.

Treat your body as a surface for transgression.

113.

Proliferate secondhand truths.

114.

Come out.

115.
Confer philosophical status on linguistic gimmicks.

116.
Scan.

117.
Milk celebrity.

118.

Lose the centre.

119.
Keep open your options for prejudice.

120.
Await catastrophe.

121.
Celebrate intensity.

122.
Blur the boundary between high and low.

123.

Watch your critical gaze slide into
ironic self-consciousness.

124.

Experiment in public.

125.

Exhibit the mark of the Other.

126.

Reconsider the artist – no longer a tormented heroic soul, but a well-heeled power broker.

127.

Speak not of reason, only reasons.

128.

Shuffle fragments.

129.

Hack.

130.

Package community.

131.

Design your own rituals.

132.

To change what things mean,
redescribe them.

133.

Don't struggle, just enjoy the
seduction.

134.

Beware: every decoding is another
encoding.

135.

Displace the canon with attitude.

136.
Misread.

137.
Purchase genuine imitations.

138
Disperse yourself in a cloud of
narrative elements.

139.
Continue the tradition of breaking
with tradition.

140.
Break with the tradition of breaking
with tradition.

141.
Follow the market.

142.
With clipped slogans and depthless
images, diminish the world.

143.

Gate your community.

144.

Vote anyway.

145.

Trouble your foundations.

146.

Network.

147.

Name what names you.

148.

Find purpose without direction.

149.

Affirm that some truth is still possible,
though a final truth is not.

150.

Fight for attention.

151.

Redeploy the images that oppose you.

152.

Study everything that can be used to tell a lie.

153.

Displace the universal human subject.

154.

Pervert.

155.

Splinter consensus.

156.

Reject ideal meanings – even the purest
ideas betray the impurities of language.

157.

Market anti-establishment postures.

158.

Care less who has power than how its effects have made you.

159.

Mix codes.

160.
Read deeply into pop.

161.
Don't probe, just indulge your
fascinations.

162.
Take pleasure.

163.

Slip into modernism.

164.

Reset your biological clock.

165.

Usurp reality.

166.

Implode metaphysics.

167.

Decipher signs by the trace of
all in each.

168.

Mass produce difference.

169.

Borrow at will.

170.

Advance science through chaos, error, deviation.

171.

Speak in a different voice.

172.

Treat history as a continuum of portable accessories.

173.

Treat history as an endless reserve of equal events.

174.

Treat history as a resource bank of images for casual reuse.

175.
Mock your own urgency.

176.
Temp.

177.
Long for a place to stash your electronic money.

178.
Approach the same horizon as the machine.

179.

Await the return of the repressed.

180.

Numb your capacity for outrage.

181.

Haemorrhage paradigms.

182.

Complicate the self-evident.

183.

Iterate.

184.

Design products with instant heritage.

185.

Unseat nature.

186.
Cut and paste.

187.
Bank.

188.
Integrate globally, disintegrate locally.

189.

Negotiate temporary contracts with
both your employer and your spouse.

190.

Tell lots of small stories.

191.

Use the word *deconstruction* without
being quite sure whether it is a rigorous
strategy for reversing the classic
hierarchies of Western philosophy
or a trendy academic parlour trick.

192.

Mess around.

193.

Outsource.

194.

Inscribe.

195.

Visit the public square on your private
screen.

196.

Expand your possibilities and your
sense of inadequacy.

197.

Accessorize your rebellion.

198.

Leave the *avant garde* behind.

199.

Do it yourself.

200.

Make fine distinctions about things
that don't matter.

201.

Collect world views.

202.

Watch all that is solid melt into air.

203.

Favour aesthetics over ethics, rhetoric over reason.

204.

Bomb smart.

205.

Manufacture nostalgia.

206.

Define your self in the mirror of the
excluded, silenced Other.

207.

Confuse the original and the copy.

208.

Write texts your readers can rewrite.

209.

Hedge.

210.

Never arrive.

211.

In wartime, watch video games on the nightly news.

212.

Expose the codes by which corporate meanings become our own.

213.

Be wherever, whenever.

214.

Occasionally pause the endless cycle of
interpretation.

215.

Make room for absence.

216.
Label your tribe.

217.
Abandon the future to fantasies of
social collapse.

218.
Buy a home built as much for fiction
as function.

219.

Saturate.

220.

Be entertained by information,
informed by entertainment.

221.

In the attempt to demystify, further obscure.

222.

Have a taste for all the world's cuisines.

223.

Imagine you're a nomadic, desiring machine, without limits.

224.

Forsake Marx, embrace Nietzsche.

225.

Defer identity.

226.

Play with texts while an oppressive
social system goes about its business.

227.

Choose religion cafeteria-style

228.

Live without a big picture.

229.

Transgress.

230.

Politicize your aesthetics, aestheticize your politics.

231.

Watch your fiercest critique become the latest rage.

232.

Switch channels.

233.
Rehash.

234
Rehash.

235.
Lower the common denominator.

236.
Open your body to technology.

237.

Be wary of stories that presume to judge other stories.

238.

Guarantee nothing.

239.

Restructure your feelings.

240.

Take irony for granted.

241.

Preserve your heritage through
aggressive marketing.

242.

Morph.

243.

Don't believe the hype.

244.

Make a spectacle of yourself.

245.

Instead of absolute truth, seek infinite dissemination.

246

Empower difference.

247.

Saw the branch on which you sit.

248.

Invest globally, deindustrialize locally.

249

Write in the margins.

250.

Read between the lines.

251.

Enjoy the confusion.

252.

Cannibalize.

253.

Pledge allegiance off the map.

254.

Lose your critical distance – an
uncolonized position no longer exists.

255.

Design other worlds.

256.

Consider what reason excludes.

257.
Change the subject.

258.
Stop making sense.

259.
Flip flop.

260.
Fall into your politics through a series of listless rejections.

261.

Leverage fictitious capital.

262.

Parody it all.

263.

Decorate your home as a sanctuary
against the speed of the world.

264.

Work without rules to find what rules
your work.

265.

Fail to say what you mean.

266.

Produce only by reproducing.

267.

Put everything in quotes.

268.

Slack.

269.

Exploit banality.

270.

Tolerate the quaint *naiveté* of those who still believe they can change the world.

271.

Forgo the desire for encyclopedic mastery.

272.

Read with an uncensored body.

273.

Question authorship.

274.

Obscure ownership.

275.

Move without changing your electronic address.

276.

Carve out one world.

277.

Use the word *post-modern* without being quite sure whether it is the dominant cultural logic of late capital-ism or pop-culture shorthand for messy looking buildings.

278.

Flip burgers.

279.

Draw your own maps.

280.

Don't write to say the last word.

281.

Watch out: philosophy is less truth than strategy.

282.

Manufacture intangibles.

283.

Discontinue.

284.

Speak with coded familiarity.

285.

Find beauty in the breakdown.

286.

Without essence or nation, compose an ethnic identity.

287.

Stay mobile.

288.

Plagiarize yourself.

289.

Be a cyborg rather than a goddess.

290.

Present yourself as a flexible, highly
skilled, short-term commodity.

291.

Use puns to subvert the claims of
seamless meaning.

292.

Play with the pieces.

293.

Tune in to a televised town hall of tasteless intimacies.

294.

Resist closure.

295.

Author your desires.

296.

See what you believe.

297.

Beware of intellectuals who speak of
Otherness only amongst themselves.

298.

Negotiate truth.

299.
Blur genres.

300.
Disembody.

301.
Advance science by expanding the pool
of incompatible alternatives.

302.

Move the margins to the centre.

303.

Break the frame.

304.

Bring back the aura.

305.

Amidst a permanent crisis in art,
surrender to the market.

306.

Review the reviewer.

307.

Buy time.

308.

Need speed.

309.

Remember: essence *is* only as
essence *of*.

310.

Populate your wardrobe with
corporate logos.

311.

Use one text to read another.

312.

Get along with each of your selves.

313.

Take casual labour seriously.

314.

Bullshit.

315.

Distrust photographic evidence.

316.

Lose the thread.

317.

Don't look for the centre of power
— it's everywhere.

318.

Dabble in schizophrenia.

319.
Simulate.

320.
From the gaps, the margins, the
boundaries – resist.

321.
Recast the familiar until it demands
explanation.

322.

Imagine contrary bodies.

323.

Travel abroad to find some suppressed aspect of yourself on public display.

324.

Replicate.

325.

Know the sacred through pop.

326.

Have beliefs, but don't believe.

327.

Let anything go.

328.

Read classics and comics the same way.

329.

Suspect your commitments.

330.

Explore the richness of your
limitations.

331.

Talk your own vernacular.

332.

Mutate.

333.

Zone for disparities in wealth.

334.

Play language games – your identity
depends on it.

335.

Code or be coded.

336.

Reschedule the crisis.

337.

©.

338.

Imitate old styles with new technology.

339.

Prepare to be misunderstood.

340.

In panicked defence of the sacred,
embrace fundamentalism.

341.

Replace your career with multiple
revenue streams.

342.

Log on to an electronic prosthesis.

343.

Make the border your territory.

344.

Impersonate yourself.

345.

Downsize.

346.

Upgrade.

347.

In an age of lost innocence, use irony to speak of love.

348.

Derive that from which you once
thought all else derived.

349.

Traffic in novelty.

350.

Launch your critiques from a position
of inexcusable involvement.

351.

Listen closely: every story is a complex
act of power.

352.
Be, like, whatever.

353.
Skip around.

354.
Hype.

355.
Dissect your intimate moments.

356.

Make the news.

357.

Reject general concepts.

358.

Multiply genders.

359.
Celebrate kitsch.

360.
Seek provisional truth.

361.
Stop waiting for Godot.

362.

Betray memory.

363.

Spawn new sensibilities.

364

Continue to think and write even
though reason is dead, history is over,
the self is fractured, and knowledge is
hopelessly enmeshed in oppressive
relations of power.

365.

Practice one-liners.

Bibliography

True to the spirit of post-modernism, this is a work of inspired imitation. Credit is due to source texts, as follows:

Anderson, Walter Truett, ed. *The Truth about the Truth: De-confusing and Re-constructing the Postmodern World*. New York: Tarcher/Putnam, 1995.

Appignanesi, Richard, and Chris Garratt. *Introducing Postmodernism*. New York: Totem Books, 1995.

Atkins, Robert. *ArtSpeak: A Guide to Contemporary Ideas, Movements, and Buzzwords*. New York: Abbeville Press, 1990.

Best, Steven, and Douglas Kellner. *Postmodern Theory: Critical Interrogations*. New York: Guilford Press, 1991.

Bukatman, Scott, *Blade Runner*. London: British Film Institute, 1997.

BIBLIOGRAPHY

Computer Lab, The. *Beyond Cyberpunk!: A Do-It-Yourself Guide to the Future* (version 1.02). Louisa, VA: The Computer Lab, 1991.

Culler, Jonathan. *On Deconstruction: Theory and Criticism after Structuralism*. Ithaca: Cornell University Press, NY, 1982.

Dery, Mark. *Culture Jamming: Culture Jamming, Hacking, Slashing and Sniping in the Empire of Signs*. Westfield, NJ: Open Magazine Pamphlet Series, 1993.

Docherty, Thomas, ed. *Post-Modernism: A Reader*. New York: Columbia University Press, 1993.

Flax, Jane. *Thinking Fragments: Psychoanalysis, Feminism, and Postmodernism in the Contemporary West*. Berkeley, CA: University of California Press, 1990.

Frank, Thomas, and Matt Weiland, eds. *Commodify Your Dissent: Salvos from The Baffler*. New York: W. W. Norton, 1997.

Gergen, Kenneth. *The Saturated Self: Dilemmas of*

Identity in Contemporary Life. New York: Basic Books, 1992.

Harvey, David. *The Condition of Post-Modernity*. Cambridge, MA: Blackwell Publishers, 1989.

Miller, Sarah. *Storytelling as Alchemy: Postmodernist and Feminist Approaches to History in the Fiction of Jeanette Winterson*. Unpublished undergraduate thesis, 1994.

Newman, Charles. *The Post-Modern Aura: The Act of Fiction in an Age of Inflation*. Evanston, IL: Northwestern University Press, 1985.

Ryan, Michael. *Marxism and Deconstruction: A Critical Articulation*. Baltimore, MD: Johns Hopkins University Press, 1982.

Sarup, Madan. *Introductory Guide to Post-Modernism and Post-Structuralism*. Athens: University of Georgia Press, 1993.

Sturrock, John. *Structuralism and Since*. Oxford, UK: Oxford University Press, 1979.

Taylor, Mark C., and Esa Saarinen. *Imagologies: Media Philosophy*. London: Routledge, 1994.

BIBLIOGRAPHY

Wice, Nathaniel, and Steven Daly. *alt. culture: an
a-to-z guide to the '90s — underground, online,
and over-the-counter*. New York:
HarperCollins, 1995.

Additional credit is due to the following authors
and thinkers:
James Baldwin, Roland Barthes, Jean
Baudrillard, Michael Berube, Jay Cantor, Gilles
Deleuze and Felix Guattari, Jacques Derrida,
Umberto Eco, Paul Feyerabend, Michel Foucault,
Nancy Fraser and Linda Nicholson, Charles
Jencks, Steiner Kvale, Donna Haraway, Ihab
Hassan, bell hooks, Fredric Jameson, Jacques
Lacan, Claude Levi Strauss, Robert Jay Lifton,
Sabina Lovibond, Jean-Francois Lyotard, Martin
Marty, Karl Marx and Friedrich Engels, Friedrich
Nietzsche, Maureen O'Hara, Richard Rorty,
Ferdinand de Saussure, Richard Shweder,
William Simon, Robert Venturi, Paul Virillio,
Cornel West.